JOURNEY FOR JUSTICE
THE LIFE OF LARRY ITLIONG

WRITTEN BY Dawn Bohulano Mabalon, PhD
WITH Gayle Romasanta

ILLUSTRATED BY Andre Sibayan

BRIDGE +DELTA

STOCKTON, CALIFORNIA

Publisher's Cataloging-In-Publication Data
(Prepared by The Donohue Group, Inc.)

NAMES: Mabalon, Dawn Bohulano. | Romasanta, Gayle. | Sibayan, Andre, illustrator.

TITLE: Journey for Justice : the Life of Larry Itliong / by Dawn B. Mabalon with Gayle Romasanta ; illustration by Andre Sibayan.

DESCRIPTION: Stockton, California : Bridge and Delta Publishing, [2018] | Interest age level: 008-015. | Includes bibliographical references. | Summary: " ... tells the story of Larry Itliong's lifelong fight for a farmworkers union, and the birth of one of the most significant American social movements of all time, the farmworker's struggle, and its most enduring union, the United Farm Workers, founded by Larry Itliong, Cesar Chavez, and other organizers."-- Provided by publisher.

IDENTIFIERS: ISBN 9781732199323 (hardcover)
ISBN 9781732199354 (ebook)

SUBJECTS: LCSH: Itliong, Larry, 1913-1977--Juvenile literature. | Labor leaders--United States--Biography--Juvenile literature. | Filipino Americans--Biography--Juvenile literature. | United Far Workers of America--History--Juvenile literature. | Agricultural laborers--Labor unions--United States--History--Juvenile literature. | Itliong, Larry, 1913-1977. | Labor leaders--United States--Biogrphy. | Filipino Americans--Biography. | United Farm Workers of America--History. | Agricultural laborers--Labor unions--United States--History. | LCGFT: Biographies.

CLASSIFICATION: LCC HD6509.I85 M33 2018 (print)
LCC HD6509.I85 (ebook)
DDC 331.8813092--dc23

Text copyright © 2018 by Dawn B. Mabalon and Gayle Romasanta
Illustration copyright © 2018 by Andre Sibayan
Cover illustration and design copyright © 2018 by Andre Sibayan
Typeset in Gill Sans by Julie Munsayac

Published by Bridge and Delta Publishing
Stockton, California

All rights reserved. No part of this publication may be reproduced, distributed, or transmitted in any form or by any means, including photocopying, recording, or other electronic or mechanical methods, without the prior written permission of the publisher, except in the case of brief quotations embodied in critical reviews and certain other noncommercial uses permitted by copyright law. For permission requests, write to the publisher, gayle@bridgedelta.com.

Third Printing, 2022

Printed and bound in Canada by Friesens

For all those who harvest the food we eat, and for my ancestors: my Tatay, Ernesto Tirona Mabalon, a friend of "Seven Fingers," my mom, Christine Bohulano Bloch, my Lolos, Pablo Mabalon and Delfin Bohulano, and my grandmother, Concepcion Bohulano. They all worked for decades in the fields of California and in the canneries of Alaska with honor, pride, and dignity.

DAWN

For my Lolo Victor Selga, Pedro Selga, Cirilo Selga, Benancio Selga, Fred Selga, Alex Madriaga, Steve Madriaga, and Francisco Padilla. The farm next to the delta housed us all. For that I'm forever grateful.

GAYLE

For my parents Esteban and Beth who gave me a chance to chase a dream. For my wife, Melanie, who gives me air. For my son, Niko, who gives me purpose. And for you ... for reading this book.

ANDRE

MODESTO DULAY ITLIONG was born on October 25, 1913, to Francisca and Artemio Itliong. Modesto, who was given the nickname "Larry," was born in the Philippines, in a village called San Nicolas. He was born during typhoon season, a time of heavy rains and wind.

San Nicolas was a small but beautiful town surrounded by rice fields, coconut and palm trees, green mountains, rivers, and waterfalls. The village was in Pangasinan province (another word for region) on the island of Luzon, the largest island in the Philippines, a nation in the Pacific Ocean made up of more than 7,641 islands.

Larry spent his childhood playing and working with his three brothers and two sisters. He loved to play baseball. All the villagers knew Larry to be funny, confident, and friendly.

Like many others in San Nicolas, Larry's parents were poor farmers who had little education. There wasn't even a high school in the village! Larry only attended school until the sixth grade. At the time, the Philippines was a colony of the United States, and the U.S. controlled the island nation's schools, government, military, and economy.

All schools were taught in English, and if Larry tried to speak in Ilocano, the language he spoke at home, the teachers punished him by hitting his hands with a ruler or worse. Larry's teachers praised the United States as the best, most beautiful and modern country in the world. Larry and his friends dreamed of going to America to see it with their own eyes.

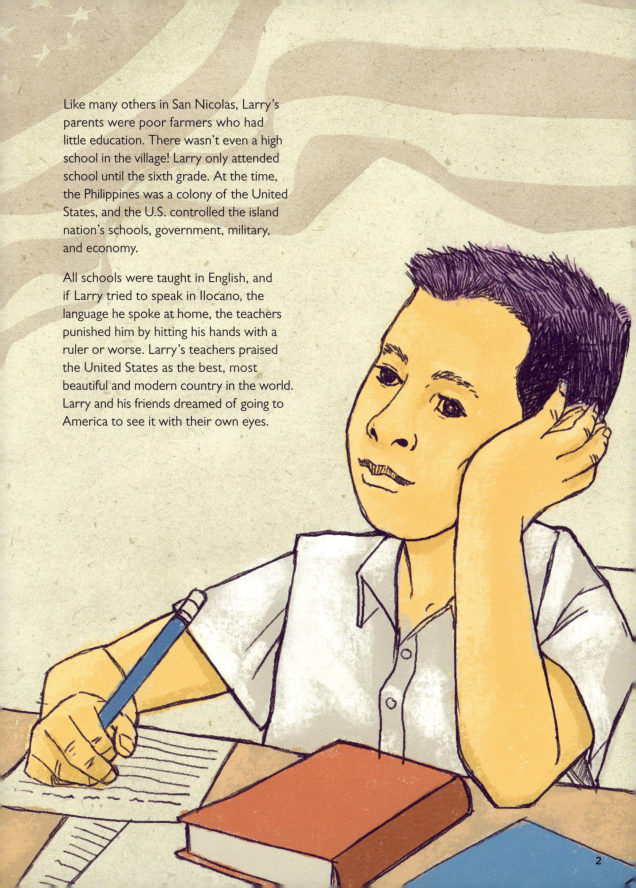

Larry's neighbor was one of the thousands of workers who left the Philippines to work in the sugar plantations and farms of Hawai'i and the United States. These farms and plantations needed laborers, and Filipinos traveled to the U.S. to work and study. The neighbor wrote letters to Larry to brag about his adventures. "Schools are good here," Larry's neighbor wrote. "You can finish high school and college very quickly." Larry liked the sound of that.

In school, Larry learned about *abogados* (attorneys, also called lawyers) who helped people with their problems. Some lawyers were rich and powerful people who represented his province in the Philippine legislature. Larry imagined himself debating with others and helping poor people.

"I want to be like that," he thought. He imagined himself with a briefcase, wearing a suit and a beautiful wool fedora, just like he saw in the photos that his neighbor and villagers sent from the United States. He could study to become a lawyer in the U.S. In his American textbooks, Larry read that everyone had equal opportunities for success in America.

WHEN LARRY WAS FIFTEEN, he decided he was going to make his dreams come true. He told his father he was going to the United States.

"Why do you want to go to America?" Larry's father asked.

"I want to go to school," Larry said.

But his father did not want him to leave. "You don't have my permission to go," he said. But Larry was stubborn, and he had made up his mind. "I'm going anyway," he insisted. "I will find the money to get there."

Larry found some neighborhood boys playing a coin game. Unfortunately, all Larry had in his pocket was his allowance— five pesos from his mother. Creating his own luck, he bet his entire allowance on the game and won 5,000 pesos and twelve acres of land! His father was angry that Larry had been gambling, but he knew the money that Larry won could help the family.

"Why don't you build the family a new house?" his father suggested.

"But my dream is to go to America," Larry said. Larry's father was disappointed, but he finally gave his permission for Larry to leave.

Before Larry left, he visited his very good friend, a classmate he liked, and told her he was leaving for America. She burst into tears.

"All the boys in the village are leaving to study and work in America. I want to go, too, but my papa won't let me travel so far alone!" she exclaimed.

"My papa didn't want me to go either. But I told him I'm going to school. I'll be back in a few years as a lawyer, and we can get married," Larry said.

"That means when you're back we'll both have our college educations! I'm going to college in Manila so I can be a teacher!" she exclaimed. "You mean it, Larry … you'll come back?" she asked.

Larry nodded. "I'll be back," he promised. "Until then, I'll write you letters." They looked at each other with hope.

Larry said the rest of his goodbyes to his family and friends in San Nicolas and went to Manila, where he bought a ticket to travel on the steamship *Empress of Asia*. All the money he had in the world, $50, he put deep in his pocket for safekeeping. He boarded the ship with hundreds of other young Filipinas and Filipinos. He quickly realized that at age fifteen, he was the youngest passenger on the entire ship! He found some older boys from San Nicolas, and they talked far into the night. Would they see snow and tall buildings? Would they find gold coins on the ground, like their teachers had told them? What would they study in college?

During the day, they went up on the ship's deck and met fellow passengers from all over the Philippines. Everyone was bursting with happiness and anticipation.

"I'm going to be a lawyer," Larry bragged.

"I'm going to Columbia University in New York City to become a nurse, like my cousin," one Filipina woman said. She showed everyone the creased photo of her smiling cousin.

THE TRIP TOOK TWENTY-TWO DAYS. When Larry landed in Seattle, Washington, it was gray, drizzly, and cold. He had never felt such chilly air before! He gazed with wonder at the buildings surrounded by mountains, trees, and snow-topped Mount Rainier. One of his uncles lived in Seattle and met him at the pier. "Let's go meet other Pinoys! 'Pinoys,' that's the nickname for Filipinos in America," his uncle said. He lowered his voice. "Do you have any money?" he asked. "I'm out of work and I could use $5 for food and rent." This took Larry by surprise as they walked toward Chinatown in downtown Seattle to make new friends and eat Filipino food. As they approached King Street, Larry saw hundreds of Filipinos in stylish suits, hanging out on the sidewalks, and talking loudly in many Filipino languages and in English. He heard one young man speaking Ilocano, so he introduced himself.

"We're Alaskeros, workers in the salmon canneries in Alaska," the young man told him. "We're waiting for the season to start. After the cannery season, we go up and down California, throughout Washington, and even to Montana, harvesting fruits and vegetables."

One of the older men showed Larry his rough, calloused hands. "We harvest grapes, onions, tomatoes, asparagus, potatoes, peaches, lettuce, celery, and more," he said. "The work is so hard, and my back always hurts, but I send money home to my family so they can live a better life in the Philippines." Larry walked farther down King Street, where he met another Ilocano. "I attended the University of Washington and studied to become a lawyer," he said, "but I had to quit to earn money. We all work in canneries, restaurants, or as house cleaners or servants. If you have brown skin, you can't get any other kind of job." He told Larry that he and others from his town in the Philippines put together what little money they had to buy food and rent a small apartment. Larry felt like he was punched in the gut. He thought, *This is life in America?*

After two weeks in Seattle, Larry heard that a farmer in Montana needed workers to harvest sugar beets. He said goodbye to his uncle and hopped on a train to Montana. There, Larry woke before dawn and worked with a crew of Filipinos who hunched over the land for hours under a relentless sun during the day and in freezing wind at night. They worked with no breaks, toilets, or clean drinking water, and they slept in old barns and dusty bunkhouses with dirt floors. Larry's back and knees ached, and his sore muscles made him toss and turn at night. He had to wear a wide-brimmed hat, long sleeves, and boots for protection from the sun and dust. He sometimes worked twelve hours or more a day and had no days off.

The farmers also used poisonous chemicals called pesticides on the crops to kill the insects that damaged the crops, but the pesticides also hurt the workers.

After the lettuce season was over, Larry found a job working on the railroad in Montana. One day, while he was riding the train, he realized that he missed his stop. With the train going full speed, Larry jumped off, but his right pinky finger got caught in the train door! He lost a lot of blood and stayed in the hospital for three months. His fingers were so damaged that the doctor had to amputate, or surgically remove, three fingers on his right hand.

After Larry healed, his friends in the United States gave him a new nickname: "Seven Fingers." He knew they were only teasing him, and he thought it was funny. He wrote a letter to his family about the accident, and he looked for a new job. Larry's father wrote back and suggested that he could go to college in Manila and live with an uncle there. Larry wondered what his former classmates would think of him. He left for America with big hopes, only to come home with nothing. Even worse, he would return with three fewer fingers!

Larry wrote back right away. "No, I came here of my own free will and if I can't lick this problem by myself, then I am nobody," he wrote.

Larry returned to Washington, where he got a job as a janitor at the Frye Lettuce Farm for 12 cents an hour. Every day, Larry watched the Filipino workers stooped low and moving quickly, row after row, cutting the heads of lettuce from the roots in the earth for 10 cents an hour.

On the farm, the white workers received 15 cents an hour for an easier job: they washed and packed lettuce into boxes in a nearby shed, preparing them to be shipped all over the nation. Soon, the white workers demanded a 10-cent raise. When the bosses said no, the white workers went on strike. A strike is when all workers agree to stop working. Together, they demand a higher wage and better working conditions. If the employer agrees to workers' demands, the strike ends and the workers return to work.

The shed workers asked the Filipinos to join them in the strike and promised the Filipinos that they would not go back to work unless everyone got a raise. The Filipinos agreed, and the next day, more than 500 Filipino workers demanded a 5-cent raise. Until they got it, they refused to work. Larry joined the strike.

"Why are you going on strike? You work inside!" the superintendent shouted. Larry responded, "These are my people. If I stay here in the office, I would be a chicken."

After three weeks of the strike, the employer Frye Lettuce Farm gave the white workers a 10-cent raise, and they returned to work. The Filipinos did not receive a raise. Larry felt angry. *We only asked for 5 cents*, he thought. He and the other Filipinos felt betrayed. And even worse, despite their promises to the Filipino workers to stand in unity with them, the shed workers found "scabs," or replacement workers, for the Filipinos who went on strike, and all the Filipinos lost their jobs. (Another word for scabs is strikebreaker. If employers have replacement workers, they don't have to agree to the demands of those who are on strike, and then the strike is broken.) This experience taught Larry an important lesson: all workers had to be unified in their fight for justice.

After the lettuce strike, Larry went to Alaska to work in the salmon canneries with thousands of other Filipino and Asian immigrant workers, right next to the Pacific Ocean, which teemed with salmon in the summertime. Standing at the edge of the pier, he marveled, "I've never seen so many fish in my life!"

Wearing long rubber boots and a big black apron, he worked six days a week, ten hours a day, cleaning and canning salmon. When the salmon were most plentiful, Larry and the cannery workers worked twenty-three hours a day with only one hour of sleep.

Because Larry was a growing teenager, he was always hungry. His stomach growled when he saw that the white bosses ate steaks and pork chops while Filipino workers received seaweed, rice, and one small piece of salmon for all meals. *With all the salmon in the place, you get only one piece of salmon?* Larry wondered.

He was shocked. "I quit!" Larry angrily told the foreman (another word for manager). He then walked three miles to the nearest town. The foreman caught up to Larry. "Boy, they want you to come back," he said, breathless from running. "They'll give you what you want. If you want pork chop, they'll give you pork chop."

Larry knew this wasn't fair, so he responded, "No, no, no. If I get pork chops, everyone will get pork chops. If I'm the only one who can eat them, I won't eat it."

Larry went back to the cannery and climbed on a chair. "My fellow workers," he shouted. "We are working and starving like dogs to make the cannery owners rich! We deserve to eat well! Isn't this the land of equality and justice?" His fellow workers cheered for him. After Larry's speech, the food was a little bit better.

When the summer ended, Larry left Alaska and went to California. He worked all over the West Coast, riding freight trains and catching rides with friends. He canned sardines in San Pedro, harvested lettuce in Salinas, cut and packed asparagus in the San Joaquin Delta near Stockton, and each summer he returned to work in the salmon canneries in Alaska.

Larry and thousands of other immigrants and migrant workers who were doing the work of planting and harvesting fruits and vegetables made the growers and cannery owners very wealthy. These fruits and vegetables were sold all over the globe. Their labor transformed California into one of the richest economies in the world. The years went by quickly. He was working so hard to survive that he forgot about college.

Through all of this, Larry was learning important lessons: workers had a right to form a union and to be treated fairly and paid a living wage. In a union, the workers form an organization whose members stand together and agree on demands about their pay and working conditions (this is called collective bargaining). They could be a powerful force when unified. Larry joined the Filipino cannery workers union and, one summer, Larry met one of its leaders, Ernesto Mangaoang.

"We have to be fighters for our people," Ernesto told him. "We have to be able to stand on our own two feet and fight our battles." Larry nodded.

"The best labor organizers," Ernesto told him, "are tolerant, fair and believe in justice for all. Be like this with everyone you meet." Larry kept this lesson in his heart.

By this time, the nation was in the grip of the Great Depression. Millions of people lost their jobs, homes, and farms, and were struggling to survive. Some blamed immigrants, particularly Mexicans and Filipinos, for taking all the jobs, even though that was not true. As he worked up and down the West Coast, Larry experienced brutal racism (hatred of people because of their skin color). Most cities and towns practiced segregation, or separation of people based on skin color. Many Filipinas and Filipinos could only live in areas called Little Manilas, or in Chinatowns.

One day, while Larry was walking in downtown Stockton's Little Manila, a vibrant area full of Filipino stores, restaurants, and other businesses, Larry saw a group of white teenagers jump out of a car with baseball bats and call Filipinos terrible, ugly names like "brown monkey." They beat up as many Filipinos as they could before driving off. In most American cities, there were areas where Filipinos were not welcome. Larry saw signs that read "Positively No Filipinos Allowed" and "No Dogs and No Filipinos Allowed" in front of hotels, restaurants, and stores in Stockton and all over California. He heard stories of Filipino labor camps that had been bombed, and of Filipinos who had been beaten. Some had been shot and killed.

Larry's heart ached with sadness and anger at so much injustice all around him. When it seemed that life could not get any worse for Larry and his friends, the U.S. Congress passed two laws, one right after the other, aimed at Filipinos. One law barred almost all Filipino immigrants from entering the United States. The other law, called the Repatriation Act, offered Filipinos a one-way ticket home to the Philippines, but they could never return. Only about 2,000 Filipinos took the tickets. Feeling disappointed and defeated, they packed their bags, wore their best clothes, and boarded ships at the ports of San Francisco, Los Angeles, and Seattle.

Meanwhile, Larry's friend, Carlos Bulosan, was writing a book about the Filipino experience in the United States. In the book, he wrote, "In many ways, it was a crime to be a Filipino in California." Filipinos could not become citizens, nor could they vote, own land, or marry whites. They were being treated like criminals in a land that they had once been taught was the greatest country on earth.

LARRY HAD A DECISION TO MAKE. Should he take the free ticket and go back to San Nicolas? He closed his eyes and imagined the waterfalls and the green mountains of his quiet village. He thought of his parents and his childhood sweetheart. Larry began to write a letter to his childhood friend. "I'm sorry, but I'm not coming home," he wrote.

His heart felt heavy as he explained that he had a new dream: he was staying in America. He wanted to be a labor organizer, someone who inspired his fellow workers to join together into a union that fights for their rights. Larry wasn't sure if he would ever become a lawyer, but he could still help people get justice. He was going to stay.

WORKERS ALL OVER THE WEST COAST were forming unions and striking for better wages and working conditions. But cannery and farm owners were powerful, and they had sheriffs, police, judges, and officials on their side. Strikes were crushed because of beatings, shootings, arrests, and murders of union members and leaders.

Larry was in Stockton getting ready to harvest asparagus in April 1939, when he learned with shock that the asparagus growers cut their wages by 10 percent. They could barely live on 10 cents an hour, Larry thought. After a long meeting, the workers formed a union called the Filipino Agricultural Laborers Association (FALA) and they voted to go on strike and demand a raise. On Friday, April 7, 1939, Larry and more than 6,000 workers walked off the asparagus fields. Not one Filipino went to work, and everyone was peaceful. The entire Filipino community supported them by cooking meals for them. The growers agreed to restore the wages because without any workers, they would lose their crop and millions of dollars of profits.

However, when World War II came, many FALA members joined special Filipino regiments in the United States Army, so the union disbanded. Because his right hand was missing three fingers, Larry was turned away when he tried to become a soldier during the war. He worked on a ship in the Pacific Ocean instead. After WWII, the Philippines became an independent country, and Filipinos could now become United States citizens. Larry passed the citizenship test about American history and became a U.S. citizen.

After the war, the Alaska cannery workers union, Local 7, decided to help their members gain better wages and working conditions in the asparagus fields in Stockton. After all, most of the asparagus workers worked in Alaska during the summer after their cannery work ended. Larry and the leaders of Local 7, such as Ernesto Mangaoang, Chris Mensalvas, and Carlos Bulosan, and Stockton leaders like Rudy Delvo, helped lead an asparagus strike in Stockton in 1948. Thousands of Filipino workers walked off the fields, demanded higher pay and better work conditions, and marched through downtown Stockton. They lost. But the next year, the union forced the farmers to agree to at least $2 an hour.

Soon after the strike, Larry's close friend Ernesto Mangaoang was arrested, along with other leaders of the union, like Chris Mensalvas. The U.S. government was trying to deport Ernesto (send him back to the Philippines).

"They think we're dangerous," Ernesto wrote to Larry, "because we want a different kind of government in which everyone is equal, and poor and working people have as much power as the rich and powerful."

Ernesto's case went all the way to the Supreme Court, where he argued that the U.S. Constitution gave him the freedom to have his own beliefs about equality and justice. And he won!

But these arrests made all Filipino farm labor organizers nervous about talking about justice. No one wanted to be arrested and deported for their political beliefs. Consequently, farm labor organizing slowed down. Larry was beginning to feel disheartened about his dream. Larry made Stockton his home base and continued to work in the fields and in Alaska. He made many friends in Stockton and became a leader in the community.

One day in 1959, Larry spotted his friend Rudy Delvo on El Dorado Street in Stockton's Little Manila. "Larry, I just got a new job with a new farm labor union!" Rudy exclaimed. "I think this is the union that will finally bring us justice! Come and work with us as an organizer!"

"Tell me more," Larry said.

Rudy took him to the union office near Little Manila and told him all about the Agricultural Workers Organizing Committee (AWOC). It had support from a powerful national union, the American Federation of Labor-Congress of Industrial Organizations (AFL-CIO). At first, Larry was hesitant.

"We've heard that everybody depends on you, Larry," one of the union bosses told him. "You do a lot of good things for Filipinos." Larry thought it over and agreed to join the union as an organizer.

Larry met other energetic union organizers in Stockton, such as Mexican American activists Dolores Huerta and Gilbert Padilla. One day, Dolores told Larry she was leaving. She, Gilbert, and their friend, Cesar Chavez, were organizing Mexican American grape workers into a workers association in a small town called Delano, four hours south of Stockton in the Central Valley.

By going to as many farms as possible up and down the Central Valley and talking to everyone he could, Larry recruited more than 1,000 new members to the AWOC. He was so good at organizing workers that the union leaders asked Larry to move to Delano to lead the Filipino grape workers. So Larry moved to Delano. Once there, he recruited two tough and smart Filipino organizers, Pete Manuel and Ben Gines.

In May of 1965, the Filipino grape workers in Coachella Valley, in the southern tip of California near Mexico, were angry. The farmers were paying some workers $1.40 an hour, but only giving Filipino workers $1.25 an hour. Ben Gines called Larry.

"We have to go on strike," Ben insisted. Larry agreed.

The AWOC workers demanded $1.40 per hour and 25 cents a box for grapes from the growers in Coachella Valley. The police arrested many of the strikers. Because they were united and the farmers were desperate for workers, the growers gave them what they demanded after ten days of the strike. The workers finished the harvest and then went north to Delano, where the grapes were sweet and heavy on the vine. It was time for the harvest.

WHEN THE WORKERS ARRIVED IN DELANO, the grape growers refused to give them the same wage. On September 7, 1965, Larry invited hundreds of AWOC members and all the growers to meet at Filipino Hall in Delano to negotiate, but the growers didn't show up. Larry and AWOC union leaders such as Ben Gines, Pete Manuel, and Pete Velasco, led the discussion in the crowded hall.

They spoke in many different Filipino languages, like Ilocano, Visayan, and Tagalog and also in English so everyone could understand. Not all the AWOC members were Filipino; some were African American, Arab, Puerto Rican, Mexican, and some were white.

"But what about my wife and children? We might go hungry!" a Filipino worker argued. One elderly Filipino stood up. "We're not getting any younger!" he shouted. "This might be our last chance to win a good wage and the right to form a union!" Many nodded their heads.

Bob Armington, a leader in the community, raised his hand. "I move that we vote to go on strike!" he said. The crowd went silent. Larry called out, "I want those in favor to stand up with your hand raised." Everyone stood up and raised their right hand in the air. It was unanimous.

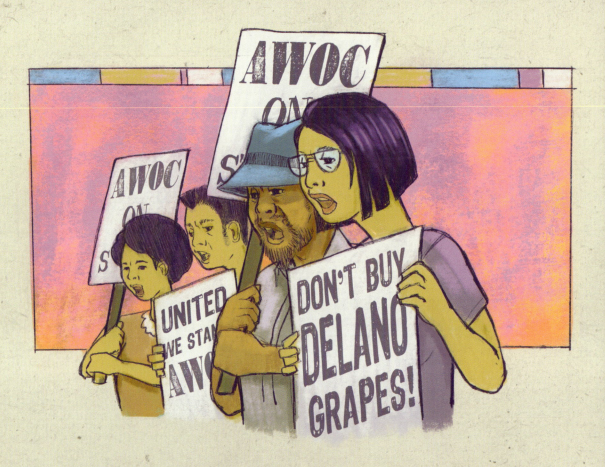

THE NEXT DAY, SEPTEMBER 8, the Great Delano Grape Strike began. More than 2,000 members of AWOC walked off the grape vineyards, leaving the grapes hanging on the vine and yelling *Welga! Strike!* Their demand was simple: $1.40 per hour, 25 cents a box, and the right to form a union. The workers walked around the vineyards across Delano, shouting and holding signs.

"For more than thirty years, I have been in strikes in the fields," one of the Filipino strikers told a reporter. "I think we are going to win this one, but whether or not we win, the growers will know they have been in a heck of a fight."

Growers hired armed guards who beat the strikers with sticks and shot at them. The growers shut off the power and water from the workers' bunkhouses. When the strikers tried to cook their meals over campfires, the guards kicked over their pots and threw their food on the ground. Next, the guards kicked the workers out of their camps, so strikers had to sleep under the trees or in their cars. The growers began hiring Mexican workers as scabs to replace the Filipinos who went on strike. The AWOC members felt hurt, angry, and betrayed by the growers. In some cases, it had been the Filipino grape workers who taught the growers how to grow grapes.

Larry had an idea. He knew that justice for farmworkers could be realized if the two biggest groups of farmworkers, Filipinos and Mexicans, could unite. He remembered what happened in the lettuce fields, when the white workers abandoned the Filipinos. For many decades, he saw that the growers made sure Filipinos and Mexicans lived in separate camps and were paid different wages so that they would always fight each other instead of the growers. He knew that if the two communities stood together in unity (also called solidarity), they would be even stronger. They might even win.

Larry knew what he had to do. In Delano, Cesar Chavez, Gilbert Padilla, and Dolores Huerta were building the membership of the National Farm Workers Association (NFWA), which was made up of mostly Mexican Americans. Larry went to see Cesar. He asked Cesar and the NFWA to join the Filipinos on strike.

"Cesar, if Mexican workers break the strike, we'll never win," Larry told him. "Then, when the Mexicans go on strike, the Filipinos will cross their picket line. The growers will always win."

Cesar Chavez shook his head. "We're not ready for a strike!" he said. But he promised Larry that the NFWA would discuss it and vote. Cesar knew if they joined the Filipinos on strike, and if they won, they would help make lives better for all workers. More than a thousand NFWA members crowded shoulder to shoulder into Guadalupe Church in Delano on a warm summer night to discuss the strike and vote. Dolores spoke first, and she told the crowd about the violent guards and how they humiliated the Filipino workers. Then, Cesar spoke: "The strike was begun by Filipinos, but it is not exclusively for them. Tonight we must decide if we are to join our fellow workers." The crowd roared. The vote was unanimous! The NFWA joined with AWOC to go on strike.

THE STRIKERS SHARED FILIPINO HALL as their union hall and strike kitchen, and they picketed together. For the first time, Mexicans and Filipinos spoke as one for the rights of workers. Most importantly, all of the strikers agreed to be nonviolent. Cesar knew that the civil rights movement had achieved many of its goals through nonviolence. This meant that all of the workers, many of whom always had to defend themselves with knives, guns, and their fists from violent attacks from racist growers and the police, had to learn how to fight for justice through nonviolent, peaceful protest.

The strikers picketed the vineyards and fields, packing sheds, and storage plants, sometimes standing on cars with bullhorns, encouraging other workers to walk off the vineyards. One of the elderly Filipino workers, Paolo Agbayani, died from a heart attack while he was picketing! The growers refused to budge.

Something had to be done to get the attention of the nation. Larry, Cesar, AWOC and NFWA, and many of the union leaders, including Dolores Huerta, Gilbert Padilla, Philip Vera Cruz, Pete Velasco, and Andy Imutan, along with hundreds of strikers, marched 340 miles north through the Central Valley, from Delano to the state Capitol in Sacramento. The sun was blistering, and their feet ached. They carried banners of La Virgen de Guadalupe (The Virgin Mary of Mexico), and American, Mexican, and Philippine flags, as well as the AWOC flag and red eagle flag of the NFWA. At first, dozens of policemen blocked them in Delano. In each town, people joined them or lined the route and cheered them on. The strikers and supporters shouted, "Viva La Huelga!" (Long Live the Strike) and "Mabuhay Ang Pinoy!" (Long Live the Filipinos). In Stockton, more than 5,000 people met them with songs and encouragement. When they got to Sacramento on Easter Sunday, thousands of cheering people greeted them in front of the Capitol.

THE NEXT YEAR, THE TWO UNIONS BECAME ONE: They formed the United Farm Workers, also known as the UFW, with Cesar Chavez as the director and Larry Itliong as the assistant director. The other union leaders included the Filipino AWOC leaders Philip Vera Cruz and Andy Imutan, and NFWA leaders Dolores Huerta and Gilbert Padilla. The UFW decided they would send volunteers across the nation to ask people all over the world to boycott (refuse to buy), grapes from Delano to force the growers to listen to their demands. Cesar Chavez even stopped eating (called fasting) for twenty-five days and drank only water to show he was willing to sacrifice his health and comfort to convince others to embrace nonviolence for social change. At first, Larry didn't agree with Cesar's strategy, and he was angry that Cesar didn't consult the union's board before going on his fast. Soon, however, Larry saw that his strategy brought needed attention to their cause from all around the world.

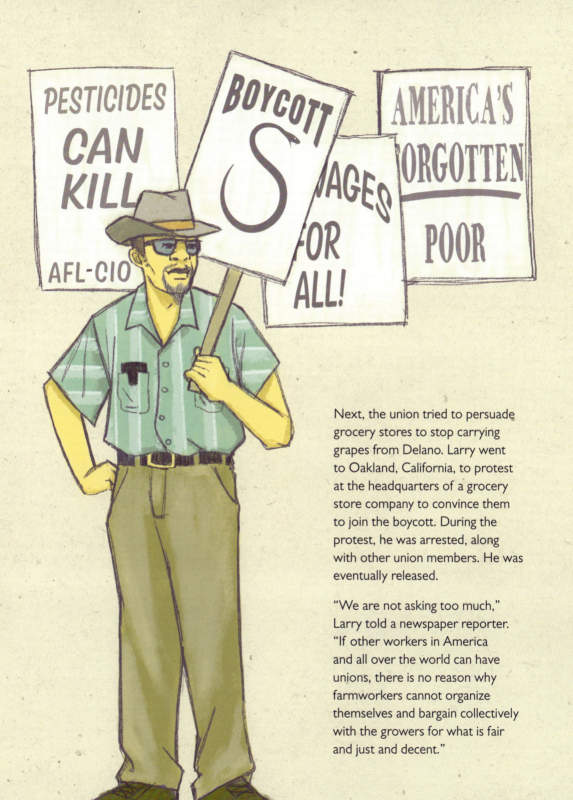

Next, the union tried to persuade grocery stores to stop carrying grapes from Delano. Larry went to Oakland, California, to protest at the headquarters of a grocery store company to convince them to join the boycott. During the protest, he was arrested, along with other union members. He was eventually released.

"We are not asking too much," Larry told a newspaper reporter. "If other workers in America and all over the world can have unions, there is no reason why farmworkers cannot organize themselves and bargain collectively with the growers for what is fair and just and decent."

IN THE FIVE LONG YEARS OF THE GRAPE STRIKE AND BOYCOTT, millions of people across the nation donated money, food, and clothing to the UFW. They began to care about farmworkers. At Christmas, people from all over the world donated toys for the children of the strikers. Filipina and Mexican women and many volunteers cooked meals every day in the Filipino Hall to feed hundreds of strikers. The two communities sang songs together, shared their food and cultures, and created strong bonds of friendship over chicken adobo, tamales, fish head soup, bittermelon, beans, tortillas, and steamed rice. The union members began calling each other "brother" and "sister." At meetings, the farmworkers did a special inspirational unity clap that started slowly and quietly. The applause grew louder and faster, and ended in loud cheers.

THE PRESSURE WORKED. In 1970, more than thirty grape growers in Delano met with the UFW and agreed to a pay increase, a medical insurance plan, and control over toxic pesticides. This was a significant victory for the union and the workers. Farmers, union members, and the press gathered at the UFW headquarters, Forty Acres, to sign the contracts. As Larry signed the new contracts, his fingers felt the rush of his signature and the enormity of the moment. He knew what this meant for his people and all farmworkers. For his entire life, he worked to create a union for farmworkers. He and his fellow workers had walked a long journey for justice and stayed their course. He had fulfilled his dream from so long ago. He did it. They did it.

But Larry did not savor the victory for very long. The work was not over yet, and farmworkers were still suffering in other crops such as lettuce. Tension was building. Larry and Cesar did not always agree on how to best help farmworkers. Larry and other Filipino workers felt they were pushed aside or ignored when Cesar made important decisions, and some of the new union hiring policies were confusing and, in their opinion, unfair to Filipinos. Filipino union members crowded into Larry's office to complain.

Some Filipinos started leaving the union, but Larry, despite his frustrations, stayed. Though he was upset at how the new union was being run, he believed in the power of a union. He had worked so hard to help make it happen, so he put his personal feelings aside. "I believe in the cause because it's bigger than me for the farmworkers to have a union," Larry told a friend. But sometimes he felt invisible because reporters only wanted to talk to Cesar. Cesar made decisions without consulting him, and some started calling the UFW "Cesar's union." Larry thought, *wasn't it everyone's union?*

BY OCTOBER OF 1971, Larry had hit a breaking point. Nearly six years after the grape strike began, and five years after the formation of the UFW, Larry finally resigned. But he didn't retire. He still supported justice for farmworkers, and he had so much work to do. He focused on helping elderly Filipinos with their problems, and he encouraged Filipinos to vote and run for office. He traveled all over the nation, talking to young Filipino Americans who asked him for advice on how to achieve justice.

At a Filipino American youth conference in Seattle, Larry told the young people, "Organize yourselves! Show me you can work together! There is nothing I wouldn't do for my people. If it were to cost my life, I'd do it. I'm proud of my people. I love my people." At another gathering of Filipino youth, he said, "What I learned is that nothing is given to you. You must fight for it."

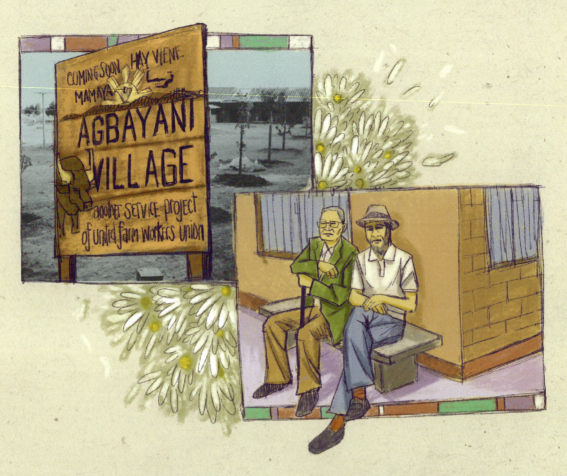

Larry worried about his friends, the elderly single Filipinos (also called Manongs, or older brothers), who did not have families or homes. Where would they live when they retired? A dream that Larry and all the Filipino workers had was realized when the United Farm Workers opened Paolo Agbayani Village in 1974, at Forty Acres in Delano.

Young people from all over the nation had come to help build it. The village was named after the Manong who died on the picket line. Finally, some of the Manongs had a place to live in the last years of their lives.

But Larry noticed that his legs had started to hurt. His doctors scrambled for answers. He was diagnosed with a fatal nerve disease called amyotrophic lateral sclerosis, also known as Lou Gehrig's disease. He died on February 8, 1977. He was only 63. When he passed, his wife, four children, and three stepchildren, along with farmworkers, union members, and the Filipino community, all mourned his death. A Filipino newspaper wrote, "His Spirit Marches On."

BORN IN A SMALL VILLAGE TO POOR FARMERS, Larry, a boy without money or power, but with big dreams, helped to change the world by fighting for justice. He spent his life helping poor people and workers, led the Great Delano Grape Strike, and became a leader in the farmworkers movement, one of the greatest social movements in American history.

Like his name implies, Modesto Dulay "Larry" Itliong was a modest man, but he was a force who believed deep in his heart that all people should have justice, and he was so passionate that he dedicated every day of his life to this dream.

MANY ACTIVISTS AND COMMUNITY MEMBERS have worked together to remember the legacy of Larry Itliong. In 2014, the first Filipino American California assemblymember, now Attorney General Rob Bonta authored Assembly Bill 7, designating Larry Itliong Day. As a result, the state of California in 2015 named October 25 "Larry Itliong Day" to celebrate his birthday and to encourage people to learn more about Larry's accomplishments. A middle school in Union City, California, was renamed Itliong-Vera Cruz Middle School.

COMMUNITIES AND STUDENTS CAN HONOR LARRY'S LEGACY IN MANY WAYS. Students can write and present reports about his commitment to fighting for equality and justice. They can encourage people to exercise their right to vote and to encourage others to run for office, volunteer, or fundraise for a cause they believe in. They can also call or write their local elected officials and support the right to earn a living wage, the right to form and join unions, the right to work without being poisoned by pesticides, and the right to safe, healthy working conditions that allow all to work with pride and dignity.

IMPORTANT DATES

1896 The Philippines declares independence from Spain on June 12. The Philippine Revolution begins.

1898-1899 The U.S. and Spain engage in the Spanish-American War. After brief fighting in Cuba and in Manila Bay, the U.S. buys Guam, Puerto Rico, and the Philippines from Spain for $20 million.

1899-1902 Official years of the Philippine-American War, when the First Philippine Republic resisted U.S. conquest. Fighting continued in some areas until 1913. One million Filipinos were killed in the war. The Philippines became a U.S. colony from 1899-1946. As colonial subjects, or "nationals," thousands of Filipinos enter the United States without restriction from 1902 to 1934.

1913 Modesto "Larry" Dulay Itliong is born in San Nicolas, Pangasinan, on October 25.

1929 Larry lands in Seattle, Washington on the ship *Empress of Asia* on April 6.

1920s-1941 Filipino farm and cannery workers, along with farmworkers of all backgrounds, demand a living wage and humane working conditions. They form unions and go on strikes across the nation. Some strikes are won, but most strikes are crushed.

1933 Filipino salmon cannery workers in Alaska, including Larry Itliong, organize the Cannery Workers and Farm Laborers' Union in Seattle. Larry serves as a delegate, dispatcher, steward and vice president. He also organizes a union for sardine cannery workers in San Pedro/Wilmington, California.

1934 Congress passes the Tydings-McDuffie Act, which reclassifies Filipinos from "nationals" to "aliens" and limits immigration to fifty per year.

1935 Congress passes the Repatriation Act, which offers Filipino immigrants a one-way ticket back to the Philippines on the condition that they never return. Approximately 2,000 Filipinos take the ticket.

1941-1945 During World War II, Larry worked as a messman on a boat, the USAT Aconcagua, in the Pacific. He settles in Stockton, California after the war.

1946 Passed on July 2, the Luce-Celler Act allows Filipino immigrants to become citizens. The Philippines becomes an independent nation on July 4. Carlos Bulosan publishes the novel *America Is in the Heart*.

1947-1949 The Cold War begins, and Congress passes several anti-Communist laws. The Taft-Hartley Act required union leaders to swear they had never been Communists. The McCarran Internal Security Act targeted U.S. residents who were "subversive" or "radical"; noncitizens could be arrested and deported. Many Filipino organizers were current or former Communists or politically radical, so these laws particularly affected them.

APRIL 1960 Larry is hired by the Agricultural Workers Organizing Committee (AWOC) in Stockton.

1964-65 Congress passes the Civil Rights Act, Voting Rights Act and Immigration Act.

MAY 3-14, 1965 AWOC grape strike in Coachella, California. Farmworkers win $1.40/hr.

SEPTEMBER 7, 1965 AWOC grape workers vote to go on strike at Filipino Hall in Delano, California. The Delano Grape Strike begins Sept. 8. The National Farm Workers Association joins the AWOC strike on September 16.

AUGUST 22, 1966 The AWOC and the NFWA merge to become the United Farm Workers Organizing Committee, AFL-CIO. Cesar Chavez is director, and Larry becomes assistant director. Larry helps to found the California Rural Legal Assistance (CRLA), which provides legal help for low-income people. Larry decides to run for Delano City Council. No Filipino American had ever run for office in Delano. He loses, but he wants to show that everyday people have the power to make a difference.

JULY 1967 Grape Boycott begins. Larry is named international coordinator of the boycott in 1970.

MAY 21, 1970 Contracts signed with several Delano growers.

OCTOBER 15, 1971 Larry resigns from the UFW.

1974 Agbayani Village, housing for retired Filipino farmworkers, is opened at Forty Acres in Delano, California. This had been a goal of Larry's and other Filipino leaders.

1975 California's Agricultural Labor Relations Act establishes a board to supervise farm labor union practices. The state bans the use of the short-handled hoe, which caused pain and injuries.

FEBRUARY 8, 1977 At 63, Larry Dulay Itliong passes away in Delano, California.

2013 The California Legislature passes AB 123, which requires the teaching of Filipino contributions to the farmworkers movement in public schools. In 2015, the state declares October 25 as Larry Itliong Day.

2015 Alvarado Middle School in Union City, California is renamed Itliong-Vera Cruz Middle School.

2016 The California Legislature passes a law that requires employers to pay farmworkers for overtime.

AUTHOR'S NOTE

Modesto "Larry" Itliong was a charismatic, tough, and passionate activist for the cause of farmworkers and all working people. *Journey for Justice* recognizes Larry Itliong's leadership and the role of Filipino Americans in the history of the struggle for economic and social justice in the United States. When Larry was born, the Philippines was a colony of the United States. Teachers and colonial officials stressed American cultural, economic, and racial superiority. As colonial subjects, or "nationals," Filipinas/os could enter the U.S. without restriction. Racist laws barring Asian immigrants resulted in a massive farm labor shortage in Hawai'i and on the West Coast. Recruiters brought thousands of Filipina/o laborers called sakadas to Hawai'i to work on sugar and pineapple plantations beginning in 1906. By the 1920s, Filipina/o migrants were going straight to the mainland, and Filipina/o farmworkers made up a third of the farm labor force in the nation.

When he arrived in Seattle in 1929, Larry was one of more than 100,000 Filipinas and Filipinos who traveled to the United States from 1898-1945, almost all young men (90 percent of the migrants were male). Patriarchal cultural beliefs mandated that unmarried women should not travel alone, and most believed that the young men would return quickly. Because of this sex ratio imbalance, and anti-miscegenation laws that barred marriage between whites and people of color, most early Filipino immigrants never married. The California Supreme Court struck down the state's law in 1948, allowng Larry to marry his partner Evelyn Wrye, a white woman, in 1955. They eventually divorced, and Larry would marry several times. When he passed away, he had four children and three stepchildren.

Upon arrival, Larry, like all Filipina/o immigrants, experienced a rude awakening: Racism and economic exploitation shaped their lives. Filipinas/os were barred from U.S. citizenship, voting, landownership, and living in white neighborhoods. The only jobs open to them were in cannery and farm work, in restaurants and domestic service. During the Depression, wages fell and working conditions in the fields worsened. Though pro-union legislation excluded farmworkers, Filipinos, Mexicans, and farmworkers of all backgrounds organized unions and called strikes to demand fair pay and humane working conditions. Itliong worked passionately as an organizer in farm and cannery work. Though most strikes were violently crushed by an alliance of growers, law enforcement, elected officials, and the justice system, Larry and the Filipino community learned the importance of total unity, overwhelming courage, and passionate dedication—lessons they carried into Delano in 1965.

The leadership and membership of Local 7, the union of Alaska salmon cannery workers that Larry helped to found, was grounded in radical politics. Many had been Communist Party members before World War II. After World War II, Cold War anti-Communist hysteria made Filipino labor organizers fear arrest and deportation. Moreover, unionization efforts were stymied by the Bracero Program, a federal program from 1942-1964 that provided farmers with Mexican laborers.

After World War II, Larry became a well-respected community leader in Stockton, California, home to the largest Filipino community on the mainland. In 1959, Larry was hired to organize workers for the American Federation of Labor-Congress of Industrial Organizations' (AFL-CIO) Agricultural Workers Organizing Committee (AWOC), headquartered in Stockton. In 1962, he moved to Delano, California, in the Southern San Joaquin Valley, to organize Filipino grape workers for AWOC. That same year in Delano, Cesar Chavez and several other activists formed the National Farm Workers Association (NFWA), an organization of Mexican American farmworker families.

Larry was leading the meeting on September 7, 1965, at Filipino Hall in Delano when the members of AWOC demanded $1.40 an hour and 40 cents a box, and launched the Delano Grape Strike the next day, September 8. When Larry asked Cesar Chavez to join the strike, a historic solidarity was forged between two groups that farmers had long kept divided. The unions merged to become the United Farm Workers (UFW) in 1966, with Cesar Chavez as director and Larry as assistant director, though Larry Itliong had more experience in farm labor organizing than anyone else in either organization. The Grape Boycott began in 1967 and spread the movement for farmworker justice across the globe.

But Larry's role, and the Filipino contributions to the strike and the union, were largely ignored by the mainstream media. "To hear [in the press] what's going on, it's done by the Mexicans," Larry told a reporter in 1969. "Nothing is done by us [Filipinos] … I really didn't mind for myself, because I don't care for myself. All I care is that my people should be recognized by what they have done …You don't have to mention no names." By 1969, some Filipinos felt invisible and silenced in the union. When meetings were conducted in Spanish without translation, many felt left out. Some felt discomfort with the social movement strategies the union employed, such as its religious tone, and the philosophy of nonviolence in favor of self-defense, among other issues. But Larry stayed because he believed in the power of a union.

In 1970, growers agreed to the UFW's demands of higher pay, better working conditions, and union recognition. However, the new hiring policies, which many migrant worker Filipinos felt were unfair, worsened discontent. Larry had reached a breaking point. He felt that the union was growing more undemocratic, with Cesar holding all decision-making power. In 1971, Larry resigned from the UFW. However, he continued to advocate for civic involvement, civil rights activism, immigrants and farmworkers, and he encouraged the next generation to fight for social justice. On February 8, 1977, he died from ALS. He was only 63 years old.

Farmers and growers still depend on immigrants and undocumented laborers to harvest their crops. Few farmworkers are in unions or covered by contracts. Recently, farmers across the nation have struggled to find enough workers because of anti-immigrant sentiment. The farmworkers movement serves as an inspiration for all of us to continue to work toward justice for all workers, with the right to form and join a union, fair pay, benefits, a safe environment, and healthy, affordable food for everyone.

The long struggle for farmworker rights is one of the most significant social movements in American history. The Delano Grape Strike and the UFW changed farmworker organizing forever by forging solidarity between Mexican and Filipino farmworkers and others of diverse backgrounds. Larry Itliong and Cesar Chavez were two leaders among many in a movement that was multi-ethnic and multi-generational. They did heroic deeds, but they were also human beings who made mistakes. As Philip Vera Cruz wrote in his autobiography, "We need the truth more than we need heroes." In this spirit, we hope Larry's story illuminates the importance of creating powerful coalitions in the pursuit of justice.

DAWN BOHULANO MABALON, PHD

RESOURCES

Brimner, Larry Dane. *Strike! The Farm Workers' Fight for Their Rights*. Honesdale, PA: Calkin Creek, 2014.

Bulosan, Carlos. *America Is in the Heart*. Seattle, WA: University of Washington Press, 1973.

Cordova, Fred. *Filipinos: Forgotten Asian Americans*. Seattle, WA: Filipino America National Historical Society, 1983.

Ferriss, Susan, and Ricardo Sandoval. *The Fight in the Fields: Cesar Chavez and the Farmworker Movement*. San Diego, CA: Harcourt, Brace & Company, 1997.

Garcia, Matt. *From the Jaws of Victory: The Triumph and Tragedy of Cesar Chavez and the Farm Worker Movement*. Berkeley: University of California Press, 2012.

Mabalon, Dawn Bohulano. *Little Manila Is in the Heart: The Making of the Filipina/o American Community in Stockton, California*. Chapel Hill, NC: Duke University Press, 2013.

Pawel, Miriam. *The Crusades of Cesar Chavez: A Biography*. New York: Bloomsbury Press, 2014.

Scharlin, Craig, and Lilia V. Villanueva. *Philip Vera Cruz: A Personal History of Filipino Immigrants and the Farmworkers Movement*. Seattle, WA: University of Washington Press, 2000.

Valledor, Sid Amores. *The Original Writings of Philip Vera Cruz*. Indianapolis, IN: Dog Ear Publishing, 2006.

FILMS

Aroy, Marissa. *Delano Manongs*. 2014: Media Factory, DVD.

Tejada-Flores, Rick and Telles. *The Fight in the Fields*. 1996: Cinema Guild, DVD.

WEBSITES

Farmworker Movement Documentation Project
https://libraries.ucsd.edu/farmworkermovement/

Filipino American National Historical Society & National Pinoy Archives
www.fanhs-national.org

Welga Project Digital Archive and Repository
https://welgadigitalarchive.omeka.net

IMPORTANT PLACES

Filipino Hall
1457 Glenwood St.
Delano, California 92315

Little Manila Historic Site
Lafayette and El Dorado Streets
Stockton, California 95203
www.littlemanila.org

Filipino American National Museum, Stockton, California
Filipino American National Historical Society Archives, Seattle, Washington
www.fanhs-national.org

Cesar E. Chavez National Monument
29700 Woodford-Tehachapi Road
Keene, California 93531
www.nps.gov/cech/index.htm

The Forty Acres National Historic Landmark
30168 Garces Highway
Delano, California 93125
www.nps.gov/history/nr/travel/american_latino_heritage/The_Forty_Acres.html

---

For a complete Curriculum Resource Guide for caregivers, families, and educators please go to **WWW.BRIDGEDELTA.COM**.

PHOTO CREDITS

PAGE 17 "Get rid of all Filipinos or we'll burn this town down," James Earl Wood collection on Filipinos in California, BANC MSS C-R 4, Box 2, Folder 18. Courtesy of the Bancroft Library, University of California, Berkeley.

PAGE 17-18 Bombed Filipino Federation Building, Stockton, California, 1930. Courtesy of the Filipino American National Historical Society, Stockton Chapter.

PAGE 20 AFL-CIO and AWOC members march in support of farm workers during the Delano strike, 1965. Photograph by George Ballis. United Auto Workers Collection, Walter P. Reuther Library, Archives of Labor and Urban Affairs, Wayne State University.

PAGE 28 Filipino Hall in 1968, photograph by Peter Velasco. UFW Peter Velasco Records, Box 11, Folder 44, Walter P. Reuther Library, Archives of Labor and Urban Affairs, Wayne State University.

OUR THANKS

We would like to thank our partners, children, and families, who gave us incredible support and love as we created this book: Jesus Gonzales; Darleen B. Mabalon, Tayondee, Nonaiya, and Caden Kelley; Francis, Ruby, Jude, Luna and Lyra Novero; Pat and Carmen Romasanta; and Melanie and Niko Sibayan.

We are so grateful to the more than 450 individuals and organizations that donated to the Journey for Justice campaign to fund this book and the first children's book series about Filipino American history. Our community's support and its belief in the importance of sustaining and telling this history to the next generation brought this book to life.

We would also like to thank the many scholars, teachers, librarians, parents, and young people who read drafts of this book and gave us invaluable feedback: Tina Alejo, Marissa Aroy, David Bacon, Joan May T. Cordova, E.J. Ramos David, Arlene Daus-Magbual, Roderick Daus-Magbual, Amianan Daus-Magbual, Rebecca Delvo, Dillon Delvo, Daniel P. Gonzales, Gladys Hess, Piper Hess, Lisa Juachon, Lorie Huertas, Johnny Itliong, Anais Mendoza Juachon, Basilio Mendoza Juachon, Emily Porcincula Lawsin, Michelle McKenzie, Ruby Novero, Catherine Powell, Robyn Rodriguez, Aldrich Sabac, Gena Salonga, Lucenna Salonga, Allyson Tintiangco-Cubales, and Mahalaya Tintiangco-Cubales.

We are grateful to the archivists and librarians whose assistance in the research for this book has been so invaluable: Dr. Dorothy Cordova of the National Pinoy Archives/Filipino American National Historical Society; Catherine Powell of the Labor Archives and Research Center of San Francisco State University; Conor Casey of the Labor Archives of Washington, University of Washington Special Collections; and Kathleen Schmeling and the archivists at the Walter P. Reuther Library, Archives of Labor and Urban Affairs, Wayne State University.